# VIOLA

# 101 HIT SONGS

Available for
FLUTE, CLARINET, ALTO SAX, TENOR SAX, TRUMPET,
HORN, TROMBONE, VIOLIN, VIOLA, CELLO

ISBN 978-1-4950-7536-0

7777 W. BLUEMOUND RD. P.O. BOX 13819 MILWAUKEE, WI 53213

Visit Hal Leonard Online at
**www.halleonard.com**

# CONTENTS

# ALL ABOUT THAT BASS

**VIOLA**

Words and Music by KEVIN KADISH
and MEGHAN TRAINOR

# AMAZED

VIOLA

Words and Music by MARV GREEN,
CHRIS LINDSEY and AIMEE MAYO

Moderately slow

# ALL OF ME

VIOLA

Words and Music by JOHN STEPHENS
and TOBY GAD

# APOLOGIZE

VIOLA

Words and Music by
RYAN TEDDER

# BEAUTIFUL

VIOLA

Words and Music by
LINDA PERRY

**Moderately slow**

# BAD DAY

VIOLA

Words and Music by
DANIEL POWTER

CODA

# BAD ROMANCE

VIOLA

Words and Music by STEFANI GERMANOTTA
and NADIR KHAYAT

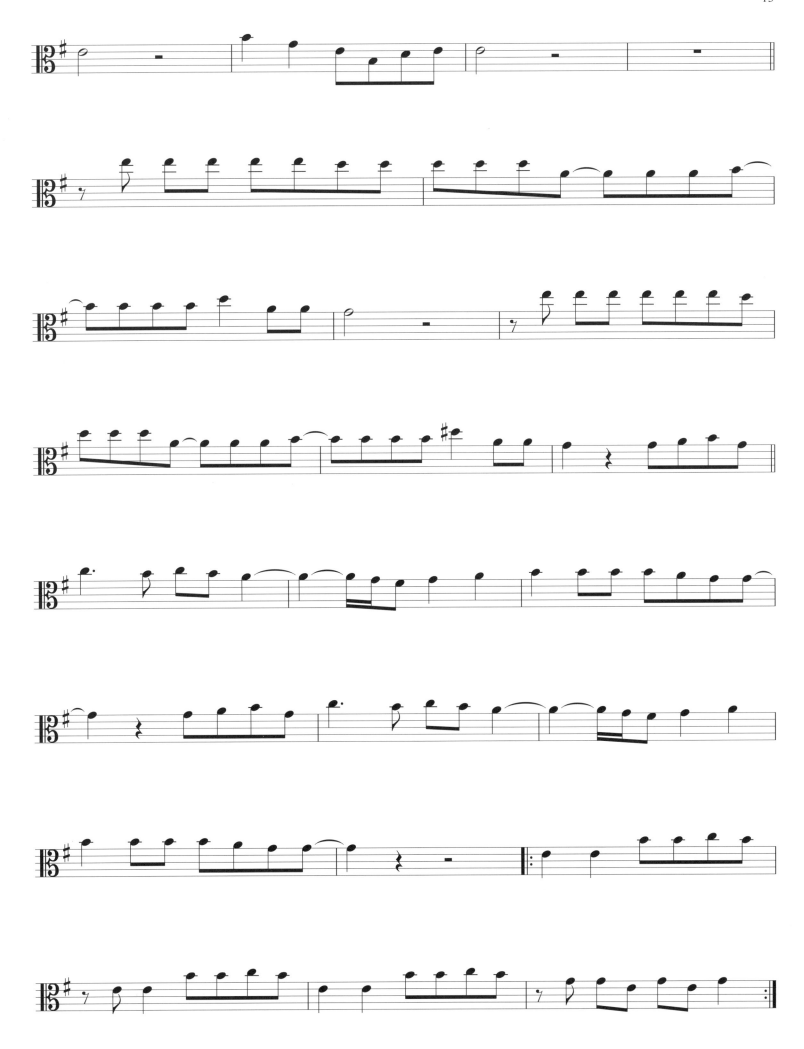

# BEAUTIFUL DAY

VIOLA

Words by BONO
Music by U2

**Moderately**

# BEAUTIFUL IN MY EYES

VIOLA

Words and Music by
JOSHUA KADISON

# BECAUSE I LOVE YOU
## (The Postman Song)

VIOLA

Words and Music by
WARREN BROOKS

# BELIEVE

VIOLA

Words and Music by BRIAN HIGGINS,
STUART McLENNEN, PAUL BARRY,
STEPHEN TORCH, MATT GRAY
and TIM POWELL

# BUTTERFLY KISSES

VIOLA

Words and Music by BOB CARLISLE
and RANDY THOMAS

# BRAVE

VIOLA

Words and Music by SARA BAREILLES
and JACK ANTONOFF

# BREAKAWAY

from THE PRINCESS DIARIES 2: ROYAL ENGAGEMENT

VIOLA

Words and Music by BRIDGET BENENATE,
AVRIL LAVIGNE and MATTHEW GERRARD

**Slowly, in 2**

# BREATHE

VIOLA

Words and Music by HOLLY LAMAR
and STEPHANIE BENTLEY

**Moderately fast**

# CALL ME MAYBE

VIOLA

Words and Music by CARLY RAE JEPSEN,
JOSHUA RAMSAY and TAVISH CROWE

# CANDLE IN THE WIND 1997

VIOLA

Words and Music by ELTON JOHN
and BERNIE TAUPIN

# CHANGE THE WORLD

featured on the Motion Picture Soundtrack PHENOMENON

VIOLA

Words and Music by WAYNE KIRKPATRICK,
GORDON KENNEDY and TOMMY SIMS

# CHASING CARS

VIOLA

Words and Music by GARY LIGHTBODY,
TOM SIMPSON, PAUL WILSON,
JONATHAN QUINN and NATHAN CONNOLLY

# THE CLIMB
from HANNAH MONTANA: THE MOVIE

VIOLA

Words and Music by JESSI ALEXANDER
and JON MABE

# CLOCKS

VIOLA

Words and Music by GUY BERRYMAN,
JON BUCKLAND, WILL CHAMPION
and CHRIS MARTIN

# DON'T KNOW WHY

VIOLA

Words and Music by
JESSE HARRIS

# COUNTDOWN

VIOLA

Words and Music by BEYONCÉ KNOWLES,
CAINON LAMB, JULIE FROST, MICHAEL BIVINS,
ESTHER DEAN, TERIUS NASH, SHEA TAYLOR,
NATHAN MORRIS and WANYA MORRIS

2nd time, D.C. al Coda

CODA

# CRUISE

VIOLA

Words and Music by CHASE RICE,
TYLER HUBBARD, BRIAN KELLEY,
JOEY MOI and JESSE RICE

**Moderately, in 2**

# CRYIN'

VIOLA

Words and Music by STEVEN TYLER,
JOE PERRY and TAYLOR RHODES

**Moderately slow, in 2**

# DIE A HAPPY MAN

VIOLA

Words and Music by THOMAS RHETT,
JOE SPARGUR and SEAN DOUGLAS

**Moderately slow**

# DILEMMA

VIOLA

Words and Music by CORNELL HAYNES,
ANTWON MAKER, KENNETH GAMBLE
and BUNNY SIGLER

**Moderately slow, in 2**

**Fine**

**2nd time, D.S. al Fine**

# DRIFT AWAY

VIOLA

Words and Music by
MENTOR WILLIAMS

**Moderately fast**

# FIELDS OF GOLD

VIOLA

Music and Lyrics by
STING

**Flowing**

# DROPS OF JUPITER
### (Tell Me)

VIOLA

Words and Music by PAT MONAHAN,
JAMES STAFFORD, ROBERT HOTCHKISS,
CHARLES COLIN and SCOTT UNDERWOOD

**Moderately**

D.S. al Coda

CODA

# FALLIN'

VIOLA

Words and Music by
ALICIA KEYS

# FIREWORK

**VIOLA**

Words and Music by KATY PERRY,
MIKKEL ERIKSEN, TOR ERIK HERMANSEN,
ESTHER DEAN and SANDY WILHELM

# FOOLISH GAMES

VIOLA

Words and Music by
JEWEL KILCHER

# FOREVER AND FOR ALWAYS

VIOLA

Words and Music by SHANIA TWAIN
and R.J. LANGE

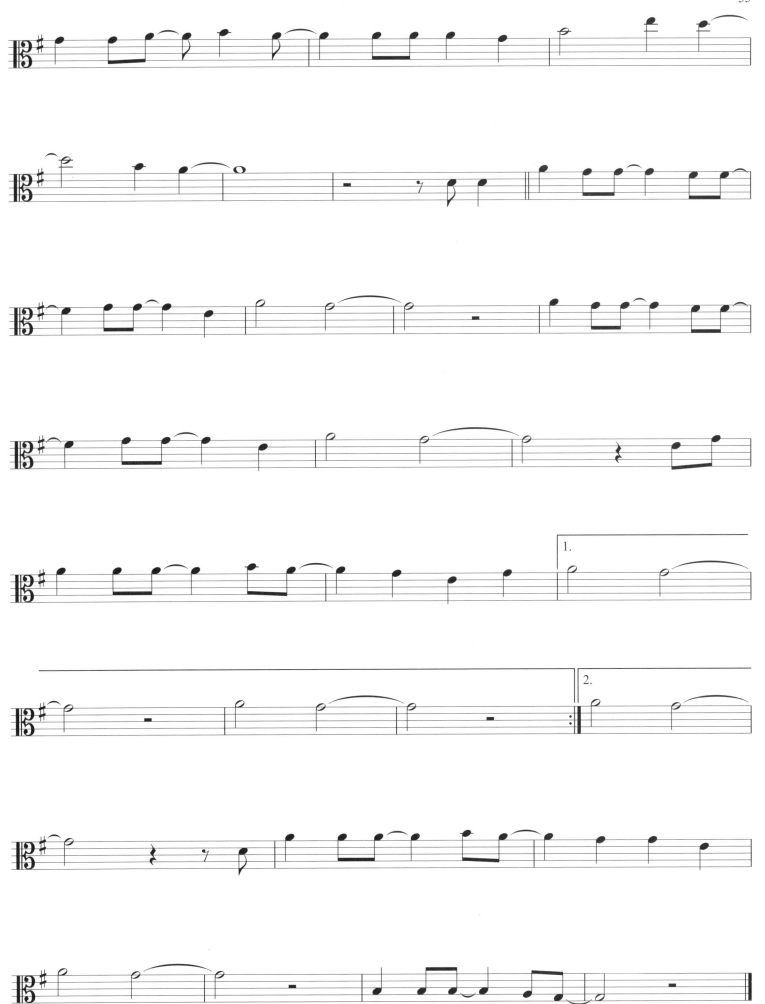

# FRIENDS IN LOW PLACES

VIOLA

Words and Music by DeWAYNE BLACKWELL
and EARL BUD LEE

# FROM A DISTANCE

VIOLA

Words and Music by
JULIE GOLD

# GENIE IN A BOTTLE

VIOLA

Words and Music by STEVE KIPNER,
DAVID FRANK and PAMELA SHEYNE

**Moderately**

# GET LUCKY

VIOLA

Words and Music by THOMAS BANGALTER,
GUY MANUEL HOMEM CHRISTO, NILE RODGERS
and PHARRELL WILLIAMS

# HOW TO SAVE A LIFE

VIOLA

Words and Music by JOSEPH KING
and ISAAC SLADE

**Moderately fast**

# HELLO

VIOLA

Words and Music by ADELE ADKINS
and GREG KURSTIN

# HERE AND NOW

**VIOLA**

Words and Music by TERRY STEELE
and DAVID ELLIOT

# HERO

VIOLA

Words and Music by ENRIQUE IGLESIAS,
PAUL BARRY and MARK TAYLOR

# HEY, SOUL SISTER

VIOLA

Words and Music by PAT MONAHAN,
ESPEN LIND and AMUND BJORKLUND

# HO HEY

VIOLA

Words and Music by JEREMY FRAITES
and WESLEY SCHULTZ

**Moderately slow, in 2**

# HOLD ON, WE'RE GOING HOME

VIOLA

Words and Music by AUBREY GRAHAM,
PAUL JEFFERIES, NOAH SHEBIB,
JORDAN ULLMAN and MAJID AL-MASKATI

**Moderately**

# HOME

VIOLA

Words and Music by GREG HOLDEN
and DREW PEARSON

# THE HOUSE THAT BUILT ME

VIOLA

Words and Music by TOM DOUGLAS
and ALLEN SHAMBLIN

**Moderately, in 2**

Fine

D.S. al Fine

# HOW AM I SUPPOSED TO LIVE WITHOUT YOU

VIOLA

Words and Music by MICHAEL BOLTON
and DOUG JAMES

**Slowly, in 2**

# I FINALLY FOUND SOMEONE

from THE MIRROR HAS TWO FACES

VIOLA

Words and Music by BARBRA STREISAND,
MARVIN HAMLISCH, R.J. LANGE
and BRYAN ADAMS

# I GOTTA FEELING

VIOLA

Words and Music by WILL ADAMS,
ALLAN PINEDA, JAIME GOMEZ, STACY FERGUSON,
DAVID GUETTA and FREDERIC RIESTERER

Moderately fast

# I KISSED A GIRL

**VIOLA**

Words and Music by KATY PERRY,
CATHY DENNIS, MAX MARTIN
and LUKASZ GOTTWALD

# I SWEAR

VIOLA

Words and Music by FRANK MYERS
and GARY BAKER

# I WILL REMEMBER YOU

Theme from THE BROTHERS McMULLEN

VIOLA

Words and Music by SARAH McLACHLAN,
SEAMUS EGAN and DAVE MERENDA

# JAR OF HEARTS

VIOLA

Words and Music by BARRETT YERETSIAN,
CHRISTINA PERRI and DREW LAWRENCE

# JUST THE WAY YOU ARE

VIOLA

Words and Music by BRUNO MARS,
ARI LEVINE, PHILIP LAWRENCE,
KHARI CAIN and KHALIL WALTON

**Moderately**

# LIPS OF AN ANGEL

VIOLA

Words and Music by AUSTIN WINKLER,
ROSS HANSON, LLOYD GARVEY, MARK KING,
MICHAEL RODDEN and BRIAN HOWES

**Slowly**

# LITTLE TALKS

VIOLA

Words and Music by
OF MONSTERS AND MEN

# LET IT GO

VIOLA

Words and Music by JAMES BAY
and PAUL BARRY

# NEED YOU NOW

VIOLA

Words and Music by HILLARY SCOTT,
CHARLES KELLEY, DAVE HAYWOOD
and JOSH KEAR

# LOSING MY RELIGION

**VIOLA**

Words and Music by WILLIAM BERRY,
PETER BUCK, MICHAEL MILLS
and MICHAEL STIPE

**Moderately fast**

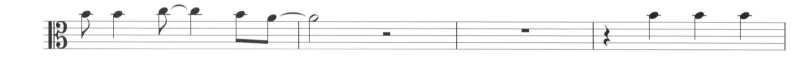

# LOVE SONG

VIOLA

Words and Music by
SARA BAREILLES

# LOVE STORY

VIOLA

Words and Music by
TAYLOR SWIFT

**Moderately**

# MORE THAN WORDS

VIOLA

Words and Music by NUNO BETTENCOURT
and GARY CHERONE

**Moderately slow**

# NO ONE

VIOLA

Words and Music by ALICIA KEYS,
KERRY BROTHERS, JR. and GEORGE HARRY

**Moderately**

# 100 YEARS

VIOLA

Words and Music by
JOHN ONDRASIK

# REHAB

VIOLA

Words and Music by
AMY WINEHOUSE

# THE POWER OF LOVE

VIOLA

Words by MARY SUSAN APPLEGATE
and JENNIFER RUSH
Music by CANDY DEROUGE
and GUNTHER MENDE

# ROAR

**VIOLA**

Words and Music by KATY PERRY,
LUKASZ GOTTWALD, MAX MARTIN,
BONNIE McKEE and HENRY WALTER

# ROLLING IN THE DEEP

VIOLA

Words and Music by ADELE ADKINS
and PAUL EPWORTH

# ROYALS

VIOLA

Words and Music by ELLA YELICH-O'CONNOR
and JOEL LITTLE

# Save the Best for Last

VIOLA

Words and Music by WENDY WALDMAN,
PHIL GALDSTON and JON LIND

# SAY SOMETHING

VIOLA

Words and Music by IAN AXEL,
CHAD VACCARINO and MIKE CAMPBELL

**Very slowly, in 4**

# SHAKE IT OFF

VIOLA

Words and Music by TAYLOR SWIFT,
MAX MARTIN and SHELLBACK

# SECRETS

VIOLA

Words and Music by
RYAN TEDDER

# SHE WILL BE LOVED

VIOLA

Words and Music by ADAM LEVINE
and JAMES VALENTINE

# SMELLS LIKE TEEN SPIRIT

VIOLA

Words and Music by KURT COBAIN,
KRIST NOVOSELIC and DAVE GROHL

**Moderately fast**

# SOMETHING TO TALK ABOUT
## (Let's Give Them Something to Talk About)

VIOLA

Words and Music by
SHIRLEY EIKHARD

**Moderately**

# STAY WITH ME

**VIOLA**

Words and Music by SAM SMITH,
JAMES NAPIER, WILLIAM EDWARD PHILLIPS,
TOM PETTY and JEFF LYNNE

# STACY'S MOM

VIOLA

Words and Music by CHRIS COLLINGWOOD
and ADAM SCHLESINGER

**Medium Rock**

# STAY

VIOLA

Words and Music by MIKKY EKKO
and JUSTIN PARKER

Fine

D.S. al Fine

# STRONGER
## (What Doesn't Kill You)

VIOLA

Words and Music by GREG KURSTIN,
JORGEN ELOFSSON, DAVID GAMSON
and ALEXANDRA TAMPOSI

# TEARS IN HEAVEN

VIOLA

Words and Music by ERIC CLAPTON
and WILL JENNINGS

# TEENAGE DREAM

VIOLA

Words and Music by KATY PERRY,
BONNIE McKEE, LUKASZ GOTTWALD,
MAX MARTIN and BENJAMIN LEVIN

# THINKING OUT LOUD

VIOLA

Words and Music by ED SHEERAN
and AMY WADGE

**Moderately slow**

# THIS LOVE

VIOLA

Words and Music by ADAM LEVINE
and JESSE CARMICHAEL

**Moderate Rock**

# A THOUSAND YEARS

from the Summit Entertainment film THE TWILIGHT SAGE: BREAKING DAWN - PART 1

VIOLA

Words and Music by DAVID HODGES
and CHRISTINA PERRI

# TILL THE WORLD ENDS

VIOLA

Words and Music by LUKASZ GOTTWALD,
MAX MARTIN, KESHA SEBERT
and ALEXANDER KRONLUND

**Moderately fast**

# UPTOWN FUNK

**VIOLA**

Words and Music by MARK RONSON,
BRUNO MARS, PHILIP LAWRENCE, JEFF BHASKER, DEVON GALLASPY,
NICHOLAUS WILLIAMS, LONNIE SIMMONS, RONNIE WILSON,
CHARLES WILSON, RUDOLPH TAYLOR and ROBERT WILSON

# VIVA LA VIDA

Words and Music by GUY BERRYMAN,
JON BUCKLAND, WILL CHAMPION
and CHRIS MARTIN

VIOLA

**Moderately**

# WAITING ON THE WORLD TO CHANGE

VIOLA

Words and Music by
JOHN MAYER

# WE CAN'T STOP

VIOLA

Words and Music by MILEY CYRUS,
THERON THOMAS, TIMOTHY THOMAS, MICHAEL WILLIAMS,
PIERRE SLAUGHTER, DOUGLAS DAVIS and RICKY WALTERS

# WE BELONG TOGETHER

VIOLA

Words and Music by MARIAH CAREY,
JERMAINE DUPRI, MANUEL SEAL, JOHNTA AUSTIN,
DARNELL BRISTOL, KENNETH EDMONDS, SIDNEY JOHNSON,
PATRICK MOTEN, BOBBY WOMACK and SANDRA SULLY

**Slow Soul**

# WE FOUND LOVE

VIOLA

Words and Music by
CALVIN HARRIS

**Moderately**

# WHAT MAKES YOU BEAUTIFUL

VIOLA

Words and Music by SAVAN KOTECHA,
RAMI YACOUB and CARL FALK

# WHEN YOU SAY NOTHING AT ALL

VIOLA

Words and Music by DON SCHLITZ
and PAUL OVERSTREET

# YOU RAISE ME UP

VIOLA

Words and Music by BRENDAN GRAHAM
and ROLF LOVLAND

_small notes optional_

# YEAH!

VIOLA

Words and Music by JAMES PHILLIPS,
LA MARQUIS JEFFERSON, CHRISTOPHER BRIDGES,
JONATHAN SMITH and SEAN GARRETT

# YOU WERE MEANT FOR ME

VIOLA

Words and Music by JEWEL MURRAY
and STEVE POLTZ

**Moderately**

To Coda

**Slowly, freely**

D.C. al Coda

**CODA**

# YOU'RE BEAUTIFUL

VIOLA

Words and Music by JAMES BLUNT,
SACHA SKARBEK and AMANDA GHOST

# YOU'RE STILL THE ONE

VIOLA

Words and Music by SHANIA TWAIN
and R.J. LANGE

# YOU'VE GOT A FRIEND IN ME

from Walt Disney's TOY STORY

VIOLA

Music and Lyrics by
RANDY NEWMAN